God's Heart To Have A Home

copyright 2023 The Burning Scroll
(Publications of Fire Ministries International).
All rights reserved.
No portion of this book may be reproduced in any form
without written permission from the publisher or author,
except as permitted by U.S. copyright law.

www.fireministriesinternational.com

Acknowledgments

Fire Ministries is a group of people whose hearts are on fire with God's desire to live in ALL of us. His love for us and our love for Him causes us to make these kids' books! Each book is soaked with prayers, God's love, and hearts burning with the passion that Jesus wants to live in kids!

I want to acknowledge with deep thankfulness the team that labored to make this book a reality. Thank you Erja Warnock for drawing images that radiate the things we read about in the Word and help us to know Jesus more. Thank you Jennifer Imboden for coloring these pictures with so much love and care. Thank you Lindsey Earles for the faith and perseverance to see it through until it reaches the hearts of those for whom it was written. And most of all, thank you Holy Spirit for filling us up with God's love to make this book a reality.

Sharing Christ with Kids

Introduction for Big People

There was a time when the disciples of Jesus wanted to keep back the little children from drawing near to Him. Jesus told them to let the little children come unto Him. Now, in our generation, we can let the little lambs in the flock draw near to Jesus also! In simplicity and by the Holy Spirit, they too can come to know Christ in resurrection reality. We should encourage their hearts to know and embrace their place in Jesus and His place in them! They may not be able to grasp these things doctrinally, but if they are born again, the Holy Spirit can communicate to their spirit and heart the reality of God's Word, Heart, and His Life (Jesus) in them.

We all must learn to come as children without the veil of doctrines and mental interpretation. Young or old, we can allow the very heart of God to be communicated to us by the Holy Spirit.

Matthew 19:14
Jesus said, Let the little children come to me, and do not hinder them, for the kingdom of heaven belongs to such as these.

Everybody needs a place to live!

But not just that, everybody needs...

a place to call HOME!

What is a home?

Home is a place you are loved!

Home is a place you are accepted.

What is a home?

Home is a place where you can take off your shoes and rest!

Home is the place where you are safe.

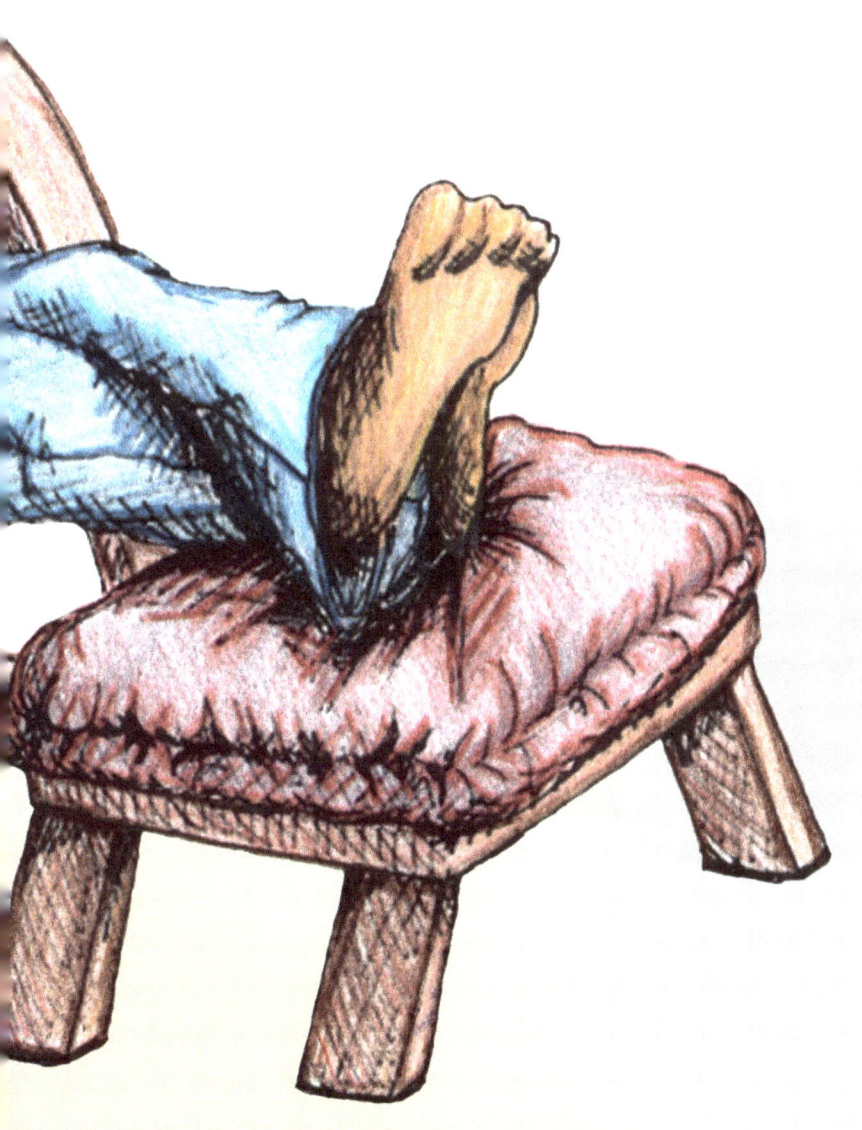

God made the heavens and the earth.
He made everything and everyone!
God loved all the people He created.
He loved them so much!

But God had a really big problem...

Even though He made
everybody and everything,
there was no place
in all of His creation
that **God** could call home.

Wouldn't it be sad...

...not to have anywhere to call home?

Luke 9:58

It would be so lonely.

From the very beginning of the earth, God would talk to people and make friends. In the beginning of creation, God and Adam would hang out a lot and just enjoy each other's company.

A little while after Adam's time, God spoke to a man named Noah and told him to build an ark! Sometimes God would send an angel to tell someone something. God would even give people dreams.

But even though God had talked to people, He had never actually come down to earth and tried to *live* here. Maybe He felt lonely and sad, because He wanted to be with us in a very special way...

Genesis 2:7-8, 3:8-9
Genesis 6:6-8, 13-14
Isaiah 66:1

Many years after Noah's day, God spoke to a man named Moses. God first spoke to Moses out of a burning bush, but eventually, God spoke to him face-to-face.

Over the years, God spoke so much from His heart with Moses, and even shared about His desire to make His home in us.

But, for that to happen, God's people had to go on a wilderness journey. So God asked Moses if he would lead His people on this adventure of knowing God's heart!

Exodus 19:4
Deuteronomy 8:2-3

God's people had only been traveling for a short while when God made the big move: He decided to actually come down to earth and land for a while! He touched down on a nearby mountain in the wilderness called "Mount Sinai."

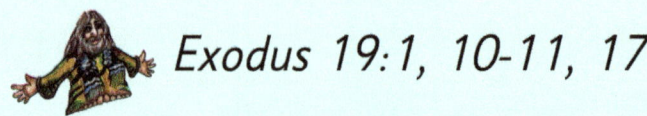 Exodus 19:1, 10-11, 17

God had never landed on earth before, and He told Moses that it would be a hard landing.

It was probably such a bumpy landing because the earth was a foreign and alien place to God.

"He was in the world, and the world was made by Him, and the world knew Him not. He came unto His own, and His own received Him not."
John 1:10-11

God said that, when He landed, there would be thunder and lightning and lots of noise and stuff. It was hard for Him to arrive here without any home to come to.

Really, there was nowhere for Him in the earth yet. This was the first time the God of heaven had landed on the earth in His Presence.

 Exodus 19:16-18

Because God had such a hard landing on Mount Sinai, the people were afraid of Him and did not want to be His friends.

They just wanted to do their chores and let Moses talk to God for them.

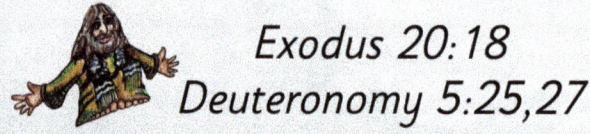
Exodus 20:18
Deuteronomy 5:25,27

Moses encouraged them not to be afraid, that God's heart was really for them!

Exodus 20:19-21
Deuteronomy 5:24-27

The people didn't really hear the cry
of God's heart, so they went back
to their own tents.

But Moses was beginning to hear
God's longing to be with us,
and so he turned his heart
toward the Lord.

Psalms 95:8-10
Hebrews 3:8-10

So God called Moses up to be with Him.
Moses wasn't afraid, and he would go up
and spend time hearing what was on
God's heart. God and Moses had
wonderful times together!

 *Exodus 20:21,
24:12, 31:18*

Moses felt comfortable and at home on top of the mountain with God. In fact, the only place Moses wanted to be was where God was.

God stayed in His cloud on that cold, dark mountaintop for a long time... but at least He had His friend Moses with Him.

Deuteronomy 5:30-31
Exodus 20:21
Exodus 33:11-15

One time, Moses went up the mountain for a very long time just to be with God, his best friend. God shared so much from His heart with Moses during this time. He even shared His desire and plan to someday make His home in people!

God gave Moses a blueprint for a home they could build Him. That way, He could live right in the middle of the camp with everyone! (Even that was just a shadowy picture of what God would do one day - make His home in us through Jesus!)

Exodus 25:40
Hebrews 8:1-2, 5;
9:9, 11; 10:1

Colossians 1:25-27
Ephesians 1:9-10

Moses wanted to share with everyone the incredible things that God had told him. His heart was full of wonder and joy after such a great time with his best friend! He was so excited to share everything with all the people down at the camp!

When Moses got back down the mountain to the rest of the people, they were dancing around a golden calf and worshiping it like a god.

*Moses was astonished!
He was just about to share
God's special plan to make
His home with them...*

Exodus 32:15-19

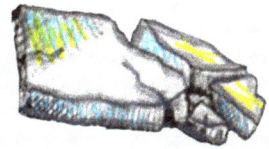

Moses had been so excited to share
God's heart and plan with the people,
but now he just felt sad and upset...

Moses broke the gift that God sent for
the people, just like he must have felt
his own heart breaking.

Exodus 32:15-19

God must have felt rejected and unwanted when His people were worshiping a golden calf instead of loving Him...

Exodus 33:1-3

Because of this, the Presence of God
no longer felt welcome to travel
in the midst of the people.

Jeremiah 2:10-13

Moses thought…

"How can I let the Lord know
He is still loved and wanted?"

Because God felt rejected by the people, Moses decided he would take his tent and put it outside the camp so that God would be able to come and visit him! Moses cared so deeply about God feeling loved.

Moses was the first person to open up his tent for God to come and feel at home. God must have been so happy! Somebody wanted to live with Him!

Just like God wanted to have a home with the people where He could live... Moses wanted God to be *his* home, too.

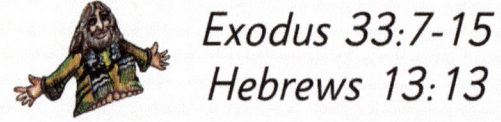

Exodus 33:7-15
Hebrews 13:13

All the people inside the camp
would look over at Moses' tent
and watch as Moses and
the Cloud of God's Presence
spent time together.

It was so amazing to watch
that all the people in the camp
would start worshiping God from
their own tents (even though
they were just watching
from a distance…).

Exodus 33:7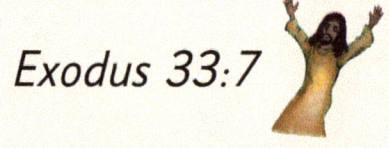

Whenever someone did want to be close to God, they would go outside the camp to Moses' tent and spend time with God.

In fact, there was a guy named Joshua who stayed in Moses' tent in the Presence of God all the time!

Exodus 33:11

Moses and all the people he was leading were traveling to a wonderful new land that God wanted to give them to live in, but Moses would not move unless God would come *with* them.

Moses only wanted to live where God was.
Moses wanted to make his home inside of God,
for only there did he feel so loved and accepted.

He did not want to live in some place if God
was not there, no matter how wonderful.
Moses did not want to move without
God's Presence with him.

Exodus 33:12-15

One time, when God and Moses
were talking on the mountain,
God shared something with Moses
that was important to His heart.
He told Moses about a certain kind of
tent He wanted the people to make.

In this tent would be a special place
where God Himself would dwell.
Though this space was small and hidden,
God would be able to dwell right in the
midst of His people, even when they were
traveling through the wilderness.

It was not the best home for God,
because He was so hidden and unknown,
but it gave a glimpse into His heart...
God was waiting for the day when He
could *truly* make His home - inside of us!

God was waiting for the time when He could make His home in our hearts...

Exodus 25:8-9
John 15:4-5
John 17:21-23
Galatians 2:20
Ephesians 2:20-22

Ephesians 3:17
Colossians 1:27
1 Corinthians 3:16
2 Corinthians 4:7
1 Peter 2:4-9

Many things have happened since the
days of Moses and his wonderful
friendship and adventure with God.

But the most important thing
is that JESUS, the Son of God,
came down to earth in the form
of a human being!

He did not just land on a mountain
in a Cloud full of God's Presence...
He came as a Person full of God's Life!

Philippians 2:6-7
John 1:17

Jesus was God's Son, and when He came to earth as a human, He showed us for the first time what it looks like for a person to be God's home! It was so amazing to see a human being (Jesus) full of God's Life (the Father).

People came from miles around just to see, hear, and even touch Jesus! Even though so many people followed Jesus, He was sad, because His real desire wasn't just to talk to us or do miracles for us... but to make His home in us and live in us.

John
6:57 10:30 12:24
14:10 14:23 17:21

Matthew 16:4
Colossians 1:27
Ephesians 2:20-22
Ephesians 3:17

Jesus knew He would be lonely and not have a home inside of us until He gave Himself on the Cross unto death (John 12:24).

When Jesus died on the Cross, He bore in His body all the "thunder and lightning" that would have come to us. Jesus paid the price to make us His home and for us to make Him our home.

Jesus died, not only to forgive us of our sins, but also to be able to make His home in our hearts and live in us.

Jesus did all of this because He loved us with the deepest love.

Ephesians 2:4-7
Colossians 2:9-13
2 Corinthians 5:21
Romans 6:3-11

God does not want to live far away from us on a mountaintop.

God does not want to be far away from us in heaven.

Just like Moses, we don't want to live far away from God, or even have to go to a church building to find Him.

We want to be with God all the time and make our home...
in Him.

Ephesians 1:6-9
Ephesians 2:13
2 Corinthians 5:17-19
Psalms 27:4, 8
1 Peter 2:5-9

When Jesus died, God opened the door so that all people could come and make their home in Jesus and He could make His Home in us.

When we ask Jesus into our hearts, we are opening the door for Jesus to make His home inside of us and to be our Life!

The Apostle Paul said, "Jesus lives in me."
Paul also said, "In Him I live!"

Galatians 2:20
Acts 17:28

God is so much better than Someone far away that we can never really know. Can you imagine how Moses felt when he heard God tell him that God wants to make His home in us?

No one loves us more than God.
He wants us to make our home in Him too.

Would you like to ask Jesus into your heart so He can make His home in you? If you open the door, He will come in and never leave you. He opened His heart to you when He died on the Cross, and now you can make your home in Him.

He is even better than our best friend...
He is our home and our Life!

Proverbs 18:24
John 15:4

Hungry for a deeper dive into Jesus in this way?

In Christ: A Place to Live

The adult version of this children's book!

available at amazon

From the Preface:

"It can be easy to hear something like "you are in Christ" and it sound like a mystical doctrine, some deep spiritual reality that is beyond our grasp. However, the Apostle Paul said, "*In Him we live and move and have our being*" (Acts 17:28). That sounds less like a doctrinal position and more like a place of life!

This little booklet is dedicated to encouraging every born-again believer and everyone who wants to be born again to REALLY know the wonder and living awe of being IN CHRIST!"

Scan the QR code to find "In Christ: A Place to Live" on Amazon!

Another Jesus Adventure for Kids!

Scan to find on Amazon!
Or search "Kelly Koshatka"
for this and other books!

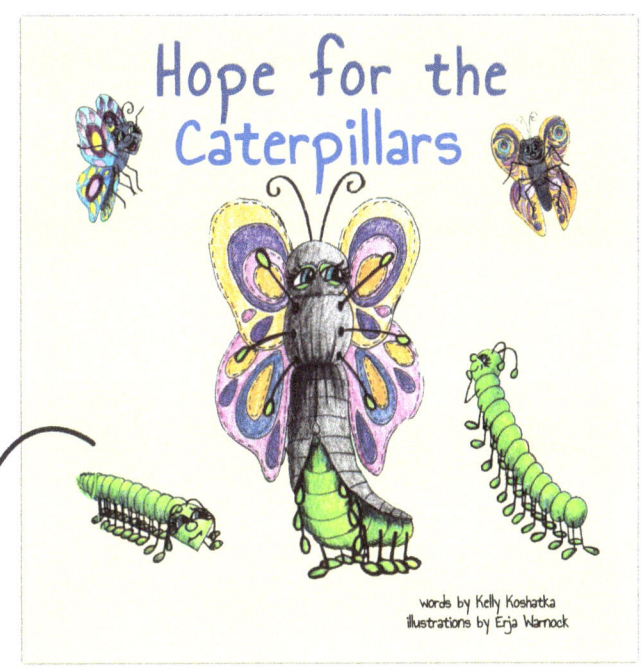

Mr. Caterpillar has Jesus living in his heart, but he still finds himself dragging around on the ground in his bad attitudes and muddy glums.

One day, he sees the most amazing thing: butterflies! Butterflies flying free, full of love to cover others, not pulled down to the earth! How did they get that way?

Join Mr. Caterpillar to find out!

Other Recommended Reading
(for teens and adults)

Born Crucified by L.E. Maxwell

The Cross of Calvary by Jessie Penn-Lewis

The Normal Christian Life by Watchman Nee

If by Amy Carmichael

the Christ As Life series by R.T. Nusbaum, including:
Vol. 1: Having the Right Message
Vol. 2: The Revelation of Christ
Vol. 3: Living in Christ
Vol. 4: The Cross of Christ

Join the Movement!

The book you're holding is more than a book - *it is part of a movement!*

The movement of Another Life - Jesus Christ the Lamb of God *in us!*

If you're hungry for more, then let's go together! Below is a QR code to sign up for our email newsletter, and we'll keep you in the loop whenever new things come!

We don't offer a "sign up freebie" or anything, only because it's not our heart to entice you like that. We just want you to join if you want to! We won't spam you, we promise. :-)

Also, if you have any questions, prayer requests, or you just want to reach out, please do! This is a two-way street!

Our email:
fromthelambwithinpeople@gmail.com

www.ingramcontent.com/pod-product-compliance
Lightning Source LLC
Chambersburg PA
CBHW061405010526
44119CB00010B/260